My Fir

Amazing Animal Books
Children's Picture Books

By Molly Davidson
Mendon Cottage Books

JD-Biz Publishing

Download Free Books!
http://MendonCottageBooks.com

Read More Amazing Animal Books

Purchase at Amazon.com

Download Free Books!
http://MendonCottageBooks.com

Table of Contents

Introduction

Eagles are the second largest birds of prey (vultures are first).

Eagles are known as one of the most lethal and vicious animals.

Eagles fly high above almost everything and use their excellent vision to spot prey on the ground or in the water.

Eagles can be found world-wide, except in Antarctica.

The Eagle is the national bird of many countries including Mexico, the United States, Germany, Poland, Egypt, and Austria.

Where Eagles Live

Eagles build nests up high; they stay there unless they are hunting.

American Bald Eagle on Its Perch

Eagles prefer to build a nest on a tall cliff, but some have to settle for the tallest trees they can find.

High nests have two benefits, the eagles are protected from predators and they can easily spy prey.

Hunting and Food

Eagles are a bird of prey – which means they hunt down other animals as food.

Different species of eagles eat different things.

They usually dive down and snatch their food, then fly right back to their nest to enjoy their meal.

An eagle with a freshly caught fish

The Golden Eagle eats mice, fish, and other birds, like geese or cranes.

The North American Bald Eagle eats just fish.

If an eagle gets hungry enough, it will eat whatever it can catch from fox to poisonous snakes!

Once the eagle has returned home with its catch, it will tear the prey apart with its sharp beak and talons.

Life and babies

An eagle couple sitting together on a tree

Eagles are very defensive and, in fact, area disputes are the reason for most conflicts between them.

When an eagle becomes an adult, it will find a high perch that it will call its own.

Remember eagles like to be high so they can spot their prey and be out of the reach of predators.

Boy eagles will do tricks to get a girl eagle to notice him. He may pick up a rock and carry it high in the air, then drop it, only to dive after it, and catch it in his mouth again.

Eagles lay about 2 eggs per year.

Golden Eagle Chicks

The babies, called chicks, will start to hunt only a few weeks after it has hatched.

When they chicks are a year old, they will leave their parents' nest and go make their own.

Some Popular Eagle Species

Bald Eagles

A Bald Eagle

The bald eagle is a very familiar to any American, because it is the national bird of the United States.

Bald eagles live close to water and eat fish and sometimes aquatic birds.

They build huge nests of up to 8 feet wide and 13 feet deep.

For many years the bald eagle was about extinct, but due to laws protecting the bald eagle, there are now hundreds of thousands of them.

Golden Eagle

Golden Eagles are one of the popular birds, used for hunting by humans.

The golden eagle is a natural-born hunter they are very fast and can kill very large animals like gray wolves.

Golden Eagle in Flight

Crowned Eagle

The crowned eagle – also known as the African crowned eagle – lives in the Sub-Saharan Africa.

This eagle attacks on the forest floor killing African monkeys, bush-bucks (like a deer looking animal), and other forest animals.

Crowned Eagles usually just crush their prey with their super strong talons.

A Crowned Eagle

White-tailed Eagle

White Tailed Eagle against a sunset sky

White-tailed eagles are very similar to the American bald eagles, but they live in Europe.

They also were almost extinct like the American Bald Eagle.

European white-tailed eagles eat anything from lambs, to deer, to otters, and fish too.

The White-tailed eagle is a little bigger than the bald eagle, because they have bigger prey to hunt.

White Tailed Sea Eagle

Fun Facts About Eagles

- Bald eagles aren't born with white heads, they are born completely brown. They have to become an adult to get their white feathers.

- Eagles have no known predators, besides other eagles and humans.

- If an eagle kills something too big to carry back to its nest, it will eat the prey right where it is or some make several trips to carry it back to the nest, in smaller pieces.

- Bald eagles can live for almost 30 years in the wild and up to 50 years in captivity (like a zoo)!

- Some eagles will pass down their nests to their chicks, and some nests get so old and heavy, the tree it's in will actually fall down because of the weight.

- The largest eagle was about nine feet wide (from wing-tip to wing-tip)!

Conclusion

Eagles are quite amazing animals.

They have extremely good eyesight to help catch prey.

Eagles have strong talons for easily grabbing and killing.

Lastly, the eagle is so wonderful, 25 different countries have the eagle on their coat of arms.

Download Free Books!
http://MendonCottageBooks.com

Top Ten Dog Breeds For Kids
Amazing Animal Books
For Young Readers
Kisha Bennett & John Davidson

German Shepherds
Dog Books for Kids
K. Bennett

Bulldogs
Dog Books for Kids
K. Bennett

Dachshund
Dog Books for Kids
K. Bennett

Poodles
Dog Books for Kids
K. Bennett

Labrador Retrievers
Dog Books for Kids
K. Bennett

Rottweilers
Dog Books for Kids
K. Bennett

Boxers
Dog Books for Kids
K. Bennett

Golden Retrievers
Dog Books for Kids
K. Bennett

Puppies
Dog Books For Kids
Amazing Animal Books
By John Davidson

Beagles
Dog Books for Kids
K. Bennett

Yorkshire Terriers
Dog Books for Kids
K. Bennett

Dogs
Top Ten Dog Breeds For Kids
Amazing Animal Books
For Young Readers
Zahra Jazeel & John Davidson

Cats For Kids
Amazing Animal Books
For Young Readers
K. Bennett & John Davidson

Foxes For Kids
Amazing Animal Books
For Young Readers
Zahra Jazeel & John Davidson

Wolves For Kids
Amazing Animal Books
For Young Readers
By John Davidson and Virginia Fidler

Our books are available at

1. Amazon.com

2. Barnes and Noble

3. Itunes

4. Kobo

5. Smashwords

6. Google Play Books

Download Free Books!
http://MendonCottageBooks.com

Publisher

JD-Biz Corp

P O Box 374

Mendon, Utah 84325

http://www.jd-biz.com/

Made in the USA
Columbia, SC
19 April 2019